Calphalon Performance Air Fry Convection Oven Cookbook for Beginners

1000-Day Tasty and Affordable Recipes to air fry, convection bake, convection broil, bake, broil, Warm and toast by Your Convection Oven

Vendy Tarjey

Table of Contents

Introduction

Technology has brought forth a lot of amazing and unique gadgets that are meant to make everyday lives of busy people easier and more convenient to deal with. One such amazing gadget that has taken the home and kitchen appliance sector by storm is air fry convection oven.

Sustainable and technologically advanced toaster oven air fryers are now one of the most sought after kitchen appliances, mainly due to how easy such a gadget is to use and the various functions that it offers to users.There are plenty of amazing manufacturers boasting convection toaster oven air fryers. However, one brand that typically stands out is none other than Calphalon performance air fry convection oven.

Calphalon performance air fry convection oven is designed in a way to reduce all your cooking worries to a bare minimum. The gadget is meant to turn even the most unhealthy, oily recipes into fun, delicious and nutritious meals!

How is that possible, you ask? Sit tight as this cookbook will guide you through all the stuff you need to know.

Chapter 1: Breakfast

Banana Bread

Preparation Time: 10 minutes
Cooking Time: 50 minutes
Serve: 10

Ingredients:

- 3 eggs
- 3 bananas
- 1/2 cup walnuts, chopped
- 2 cups almond flour
- 1 tsp baking soda
- 4 tbsp olive oil

Directions:

1. Grease loaf pan with butter and set aside.
2. Add all ingredients except walnut into the food processor and process until combined. Add walnut and stir well.
3. Pour batter into the loaf pan.
4. Place loaf pan on a wire rack in the oven and bake at 350 F for 50 minutes.
5. Slices and serve.

Nutritional Value (Amount per Serving):

- Calories 271
- Fat 21.4 g
- Carbohydrates 13.6 g
- Sugar 4.5 g
- Protein 8.4 g
- Cholesterol 49 mg

Baked Egg Muffins

Preparation Time: 10 minutes
Cooking Time: 20 minutes
Serve: 12

Ingredients:

- 12 eggs
- 1/2 cup milk
- 1/4 tsp garlic powder
- 1/2 cup ham, diced
- 1/2 cup cheddar cheese, shredded
- Pepper
- Salt

Directions:

1. Spray 12-cups muffin pan with cooking spray and set aside.
2. In a bowl, whisk eggs with milk, garlic powder, pepper, and salt. Add ham and cheese and stir well.
3. Pour egg mixture into the prepared muffin pan.
4. Place baking dish on a wire rack in the oven and bake at 375 F for 20 minutes.
5. Serve and enjoy.

Nutritional Value (Amount per Serving):

- Calories 114
- Fat 8.8 g
- Carbohydrates 1.2 g
- Sugar 0.7 g
- Protein 7.9 g
- Cholesterol 172 mg

Blueberry Oatmeal

Preparation Time: 10 minutes
Cooking Time: 20 minutes
Serve: 6

Ingredients:

- 1 egg
- 1 1/2 cups milk
- 1 cup strawberries, sliced
- 1 cup blueberries
- 2 cups old fashioned oats
- 1 1/2 tsp baking powder
- 1/4 cup maple syrup
- 1/2 tsp salt

Directions:

1. In a bowl, mix oats, salt, and baking powder.
2. Add egg, vanilla, maple syrup, and milk and stir well.
3. Add strawberries and blueberries and stir well.
4. Pour mixture into the greased baking dish.
5. Place baking dish on a wire rack in the oven and bake at 375 F for 20 minutes.
6. Serve and enjoy.

Nutritional Value (Amount per Serving):

- Calories 413
- Fat 18.7 g
- Carbohydrates 53.9 g
- Sugar 14.9 g
- Protein 9.3 g
- Cholesterol 27 mg

Italian Frittata

Preparation Time: 10 minutes
Cooking Time: 20 minutes
Serve: 4

Ingredients:

- 8 eggs
- 2 small zucchini, chopped and cooked
- 1/2 cup bacon, chopped and cooked
- 1 tbsp fresh parsley, chopped
- 3 tbsp parmesan cheese, grated
- Pepper
- Salt

Directions:

1. Spray a baking dish with cooking spray and set aside.
2. In a bowl, whisk eggs with pepper and salt.
3. Add parsley, cheese, zucchini, and bacon and stir well.
4. Pour egg mixture into the prepared baking dish.
5. Place baking dish on a wire rack in the oven and bake at 350 F for 20 minutes.
6. Serve and enjoy.

Nutritional Value (Amount per Serving):

- Calories 327
- Fat 23.2 g
- Carbohydrates 3.5 g
- Sugar 1.7 g
- Protein 26 g
- Cholesterol 367 mg

Tasty Baked Eggs

Preparation Time: 10 minutes
Cooking Time: 45 minutes
Serve: 8

Ingredients:

- 12 eggs
- 16 oz cheddar cheese, shredded
- 1/2 cup all-purpose flour
- 16 oz cottage cheese
- 1 tsp salt

Directions:

1. Grease 9*13-inch baking pan with butter and set aside.
2. In a bowl, whisk eggs with flour, cottage cheese, cheddar cheese, and salt.
3. Pour egg mixture into the prepared baking pan.
4. Place baking pan on a wire rack in the oven and bake at 350 F for 45 minutes.
5. Serve and enjoy.

Nutritional Value (Amount per Serving):

- Calories 402
- Fat 26.5 g
- Carbohydrates 9.3 g
- Sugar 1 g
- Protein 31 g
- Cholesterol 310 mg

Ham Egg Casserole

Preparation Time: 10 minutes
Cooking Time: 20 minutes
Serve: 2

Ingredients:

- 5 eggs, lightly beaten
- 1/2 cup cheddar cheese, shredded
- 1/3 cup heavy cream
- 2 green onion, chopped
- 1 slice bread, cut into pieces
- 1/3 cup ham, diced
- 1 tbsp pimento, diced
- 1/4 tsp black pepper
- 1/4 tsp salt

Directions:

1. Add bread pieces to the bottom of the greased casserole dish.
2. In a bowl, whisk eggs with heavy cream, pimento, green onion, pepper, and salt.
3. Pour egg mixture over bread. Sprinkle ham and cheese over egg mixture.
4. Place baking dish on a wire rack in the oven and bake at 350 F for 20 minutes.
5. Serve and enjoy.

Nutritional Value (Amount per Serving):

- Calories 413
- Fat 30 g
- Carbohydrates 10.7 g
- Sugar 4.6 g
- Protein 26.3 g
- Cholesterol 479 mg

Pumpkin Bread

Preparation Time: 10 minutes
Cooking Time: 35 minutes
Serve: 8

Ingredients:

- 2 eggs
- 1/4 cup coconut flour
- 1 tsp pumpkin pie spice
- 1/4 cup chocolate chips
- 1/2 cup pumpkin puree
- 1/4 cup flax seed meal
- 1/4 cup Swerve
- 1 tsp baking powder

Directions:

1. Grease loaf pan with and set aside.
2. Add all dry ingredients into the bowl and mix well. Set aside.
3. In a medium bowl, whisk pumpkin puree and eggs.
4. Pour wet ingredients mixture into the dry ingredients and mix until just combined.
5. Pour batter into the prepared loaf pan.
6. Place loaf pan on a wire rack in the oven and bake at 350 F for 35 minutes.
7. Slice and serve.

Nutritional Value (Amount per Serving):

- Calories 69
- Fat 3.8 g
- Carbohydrates 5.9 g
- Sugar 3.4 g
- Protein 2.6 g
- Cholesterol 42 mg

Broccoli Quiche

Preparation Time: 10 minutes
Cooking Time: 45 minutes
Serve: 8

Ingredients:

- 2 eggs
- 1/2 cup onion, chopped
- 1 1/2 cups milk
- 1 tsp baking powder
- 2 1/2 cups broccoli, cooked & chopped
- 8 oz cheddar cheese, shredded
- 1 cup flour
- 1 tsp salt

Directions:

1. In a bowl, mix flour, baking powder, and salt and set aside.
2. In a medium bowl, whisk eggs. Add onion and stir well.
3. Pour egg mixture into the flour mixture and stir to combine. Stir in broccoli and cheese.
4. Pour egg mixture into the greased 9-inch pie dish.
5. Place pie dish on a wire rack in the oven and bake at 350 F for 45 minutes.
6. Serve and enjoy.

Nutritional Value (Amount per Serving):

- Calories 225
- Fat 11.7 g
- Carbohydrates 17.5 g
- Sugar 3.1 g
- Protein 12.4 g
- Cholesterol 74 mg

Oat Squash Muffins

Preparation Time: 10 minutes
Cooking Time: 20 minutes
Serve: 12

Ingredients:

- 2 eggs
- 1 cup oats
- 1 cup all-purpose flour
- 1 tsp vanilla
- 1/3 cup olive oil
- 1/2 cup yogurt
- 1 tbsp pumpkin pie spice
- 2 tsp baking powder
- 1/2 cup maple syrup
- 1 cup butternut squash puree
- 1/2 tsp sea salt

Directions:

1. Line 12 cups muffin pan with cupcake liners.
2. In a bowl, whisk together eggs, vanilla, oil, yogurt, maple syrup, and squash puree.
3. In a small bowl, mix flour, pumpkin pie spice, baking powder, oats, and salt.
4. Add flour mixture into the wet mixture and stir to combine.
5. Pour batter into the prepared muffin pan.
6. Place muffin pan on a wire rack in the oven and bake at 390 F for 20 minutes.
7. Serve and enjoy.

Nutritional Value (Amount per Serving):

- Calories 171
- Fat 7.1 g
- Carbohydrates 23.8 g
- Sugar 9.4 g

- Protein 3.6 g
- Cholesterol 28 mg

Egg Cheese Casserole

Preparation Time: 10 minutes
Cooking Time: 40 minutes
Serve: 10

Ingredients:

- 12 eggs
- 1/3 cup milk
- 8 oz cheddar cheese, shredded
- 1/4 tsp pepper
- 1 tsp salt

Directions:

1. Spray 9*13-inch casserole dish with cooking spray and set aside.
2. In a bowl, whisk eggs with milk, pepper, and salt. Add shredded cheese and stir well.
3. Pour egg mixture into the prepared casserole dish.
4. Place baking dish on a wire rack in the oven and bake at 350 F for 40 minutes.
5. Serve and enjoy.

Nutritional Value (Amount per Serving):

- Calories 171
- Fat 12.9 g
- Carbohydrates 1.1 g
- Sugar 0.9 g
- Protein 12.6 g
- Cholesterol 221 mg

Chapter 2: Poultry

Meatballs

Preparation Time: 10 minutes
Cooking Time: 25 minutes
Serve: 4

Ingredients:

- 1 lb ground chicken
- 1 egg, lightly beaten
- 2 tbsp olive oil
- 1 tbsp parsley, chopped
- 1/2 cup breadcrumbs
- 1/2 cup parmesan cheese, grated
- 1/4 tsp red pepper flakes
- 1/2 tsp dried oregano
- 1 tsp dried onion flakes
- 1 garlic clove, minced
- 1/4 tsp pepper
- 1/2 tsp sea salt

Directions:

1. Add all ingredients into the mixing bowl and mix until well combined.
2. Make balls from the meat mixture and arrange on a mesh tray and bake at 390 F for 25 minutes.
3. Serve and enjoy.

Nutritional Value (Amount per Serving):

- Calories 385
- Fat 19.7 g
- Carbohydrates 11.1 g
- Sugar 1.1 g

- Protein 39.8 g
- Cholesterol 150 mg

Baked Chicken Breasts

Preparation Time: 10 minutes
Cooking Time: 20 minutes
Serve: 6

Ingredients:

- 6 chicken breasts, skinless & boneless
- 2 tbsp olive oil
- 1/4 tsp pepper
- 1/2 tsp seasoning salt
- 1/4 tsp paprika
- 1 tsp Italian seasoning

Directions:

1. Brush chicken with oil and season with paprika, Italian seasoning, pepper, and salt.
2. Place chicken breasts in a mesh basket.
3. Place mesh basket in the oven and bake at 400 F for 20 minutes.
4. Serve and enjoy.

Nutritional Value (Amount per Serving):

- Calories 320
- Fat 15.7 g
- Carbohydrates 0.2 g
- Sugar 0.1 g
- Protein 42.3 g
- Cholesterol 130 mg

Chicken Patties

Preparation Time: 10 minutes
Cooking Time: 25 minutes
Serve: 4

Ingredients:

- 1 egg
- 1 lb ground chicken
- 1/2 cup mozzarella cheese, grated cheese
- 1 cup carrot, grated
- 1 cup cauliflower, grated
- 1 tsp garlic, minced
- 1/2 cup onion, minced
- 3/4 cup breadcrumbs
- 1/8 tsp pepper
- 3/4 tsp salt

Directions:

1. Add all ingredients into the mixing bowl and mix until well combined.
2. Make patties from meat mixture and place on a mesh tray and bake at 400 F for 25 minutes.
3. Serve and enjoy.

Nutritional Value (Amount per Serving):

- Calories 346
- Fat 11.2 g
- Carbohydrates 20.4 g
- Sugar 3.9 g
- Protein 38.8 g
- Cholesterol 144 mg

Turkey Meatballs

Preparation Time: 10 minutes
Cooking Time: 25 minutes
Serve: 6

Ingredients:

- 2 eggs
- 2 lbs ground turkey
- 1/2 cup breadcrumbs
- 1 tsp cumin
- 1/2 cup parsley, chopped
- 1/2 cup onion, minced
- 1 tbsp garlic, minced
- 1/2 tsp pepper
- 1 tsp oregano
- 1/2 tsp pepper
- 1 tsp fresh mint, chopped
- 1 tsp salt

Directions:

1. Add all ingredients into the bowl and mix until well combined.
2. Make small balls from the meat mixture and place on a mesh tray and bake at 375 F for 25 minutes.
3. Serve and enjoy.

Nutritional Value (Amount per Serving):

- Calories 362
- Fat 18.7 g
- Carbohydrates 8.8 g
- Sugar 1.2 g
- Protein 44.9 g
- Cholesterol 209 mg

Tarragon Chicken

Preparation Time: 10 minutes
Cooking Time: 12 minutes
Serve: 2

Ingredients:

- 2 chicken breasts, skinless and boneless
- 1/4 cup dried tarragon
- 1 tbsp butter
- Pepper
- Salt

Directions:

1. Season chicken with pepper and salt and coat with butter.
2. Sprinkle chicken with tarragon and place on a mesh tray and bake at 390 F for 12 minutes.
3. Serve and enjoy.

Nutritional Value (Amount per Serving):

- Calories 339
- Fat 16.8 g
- Carbohydrates 1.8 g
- Sugar 0 g
- Protein 43.1 g
- Cholesterol 145 mg

Dijon Chicken Thighs

Preparation Time: 5 minutes
Cooking Time: 50 minutes
Serve: 4

Ingredients:

- 1 1/2 lbs chicken thighs, skinless and boneless
- 4 tbsp maple syrup
- 2 tsp olive oil
- 2 tbsp Dijon mustard
- 1/4 cup French mustard

Directions:

1. In a bowl, mix maple syrup, olive oil, Dijon mustard, and French mustard.
2. Add chicken to the bowl and mix until chicken is well coated with maple mixture.
3. Arrange chicken in a baking dish.
4. Place baking dish on a wire rack in the oven and bake at 375 F for 50 minutes.
5. Serve and enjoy.

Nutritional Value (Amount per Serving):

- Calories 401
- Fat 15.3 g
- Carbohydrates 13.8 g
- Sugar 12 g
- Protein 49.6 g
- Cholesterol 151 mg

Lemon Pepper Chicken

Preparation Time: 10 minutes
Cooking Time: 35 minutes
Serve: 4

Ingredients:

- 4 chicken thighs
- 2 tbsp fresh lemon juice
- 1/2 tsp paprika
- 1 tsp garlic powder
- 1/2 tsp onion powder
- 1 tbsp lemon pepper seasoning
- 2 tbsp olive oil
- 1 tsp salt

Directions:

1. Add chicken to the mixing bowl.
2. Pour lemon juice and olive oil over chicken and coat well.
3. Mix lemon pepper seasoning, paprika, Italian seasoning, onion powder, garlic powder, and salt and rub all over the chicken thighs.
4. Place chicken in baking dish.
5. Place baking dish on a wire rack in the oven and bake at 400 F for 35 minutes.
6. Serve and enjoy.

Nutritional Value (Amount per Serving):

- Calories 184
- Fat 11.6 g
- Carbohydrates 2.1 g
- Sugar 0.5 g
- Protein 17.8 g
- Cholesterol 53 mg

Baked Turkey Breast

Preparation Time: 5 minutes
Cooking Time: 45 minutes
Serve: 4

Ingredients:

- 1 lb turkey breast, cut into 1-inch cubes
- 2 tbsp olive oil
- 1 cup mushrooms, cleaned
- 1 tsp garlic powder
- 1/2 lb Brussels sprouts, cut in half
- Pepper
- Salt

Directions:

1. In a small bowl, mix oil, garlic powder, pepper, and salt.
2. In a baking dish, mix turkey, mushrooms, and Brussels sprouts. Pour oil mixture on top.
3. Place baking dish on a wire rack in the oven and bake at 350 F for 45 minutes.
4. Serve and enjoy.

Nutritional Value (Amount per Serving):

- Calories 209
- Fat 9.1 g
- Carbohydrates 11 g
- Sugar 5.7 g
- Protein 22 g
- Cholesterol 49 mg

Chili Garlic Chicken Wings

Preparation Time: 5 minutes
Cooking Time: 60 minutes
Serve: 4

Ingredients:

- 2 lbs chicken wings
- 1/2 cup coconut flour
- 1/4 tsp garlic powder
- 1/4 tsp chili powder
- 1/8 tsp paprika
- 2 tsp seasoned salt

Directions:

1. In a bowl, add all ingredients except chicken wings and mix well.
2. Add chicken wings to the bowl and coat well and place on a mesh tray and bake at 400 F for 60 minutes.
3. Serve and enjoy.

Nutritional Value (Amount per Serving):

- Calories 492
- Fat 18.4 g
- Carbohydrates 10.3 g
- Sugar 0.1 g
- Protein 67.7 g
- Cholesterol 202 mg

Chicken Casserole

Preparation Time: 5 minutes
Cooking Time: 15 minutes
Serve: 4

Ingredients:

- 1 lb cooked chicken, shredded
- 1 bell pepper, sliced
- 1/3 cup mayonnaise
- 7 oz cream cheese
- 7 oz shredded cheese
- 2 tbsp tex-mix seasoning
- 1 onion, sliced
- Pepper
- Salt

Directions:

1. Spray a baking dish with butter and set aside.
2. Mix all ingredients except 2 oz shredded cheese in a prepared baking dish. Spread remaining cheese on top.
3. Place baking dish on a wire rack and bake at 400 F for 15 minutes.
4. Serve and enjoy.

Nutritional Value (Amount per Serving):

- Calories 641
- Fat 43.8 g
- Carbohydrates 11.5 g
- Sugar 4.3 g
- Protein 49.7 g
- Cholesterol 199 mg

Chapter 3: Beef, Pork & Lamb

Meatballs

Preparation Time: 10 minutes
Cooking Time: 20 minutes
Serve: 6

Ingredients:

- 2 lbs ground beef
- 1 egg, lightly beaten
- 1 tsp oregano
- 1 tsp cinnamon
- 2 tsp cumin
- 2 tsp coriander
- 1 tsp garlic, minced
- 1 small onion, grated
- 1 tbsp fresh mint, chopped
- 1/4 cup fresh parsley, minced
- 1/2 tsp allspice
- 1 tsp paprika
- Pepper
- Salt

Directions:

1. Insert wire rack in rack position 6. Select bake, set temperature 390 F, timer for 20 minutes. Press start to preheat the oven.
2. Add all ingredients into the large mixing bowl and mix until well combined.
3. Make small balls from the meat mixture and place them on a baking sheet and bake for 20 minutes.
4. Serve and enjoy.

Nutritional Value (Amount per Serving):

- Calories 304
- Fat 10.4 g
- Carbohydrates 2.7 g
- Sugar 10.7 g
- Protein 47.3 g
- Cholesterol 162 mg

Basil Pepper Beef

Preparation Time: 10 minutes
Cooking Time: 6 hours
Serve: 6

Ingredients:

- 2 lbs stew beef, cut into 1-inch cubes
- 1 tsp dried basil
- 1 tsp dried oregano
- 1 onion, diced
- 1 1/2 cups marinara sauce
- 12 oz roasted red peppers, drained and sliced
- 12 oz artichoke hearts, drained

Directions:

1. Insert wire rack in rack position 8. Select slow cook, Set LOW for 6 hours. Press start to preheat the oven.
2. Add all ingredients into the dutch oven and stir well.
3. Cover the dutch oven with lid and cook on low for 6 hours.
4. Serve and enjoy.

Nutritional Value (Amount per Serving):

- Calories 345
- Fat 12 g
- Carbohydrates 23 g
- Sugar 11.2 g
- Protein 37 g
- Cholesterol 2 mg

Balsamic Braised Beef

Preparation Time: 10 minutes
Cooking Time: 2 hours 30 minutes
Serve: 6

Ingredients:

- 2 1/2 lbs beef chuck shoulder pot roast, boneless
- 1/4 cup dates, pitted and chopped
- 2 tbsp olive oil
- 1/4 cup flour
- 4 medium shallots, sliced
- 1 medium onion, sliced
- 1/4 cup balsamic vinegar
- 1/4 tsp pepper
- 1/2 tsp salt

Directions:

1. Insert wire rack in rack position 6. Select bake, set temperature 325 F, timer for 2 hours 30 minutes. Press start to preheat the oven.
2. Coat beef with flour.
3. Heat oil in a Dutch oven over medium heat.
4. Add meat and cook until brown. Remove meat from the Dutch oven.
5. Add vinegar and 1 1/2 cups water to the Dutch oven and stir well.
6. Return meat to the Dutch oven along with shallots, onions, dates, pepper, and salt.
7. Cover and cook in the oven for 2 hours 30 minutes or until meat is tender.
8. Serve and enjoy.

Nutritional Value (Amount per Serving):

- Calories 169
- Fat 9 g
- Carbohydrates 12.5 g
- Sugar 5.5 g

- Protein 9.9 g
- Cholesterol 29 mg

Baked Lamb Patties

Preparation Time: 10 minutes
Cooking Time: 8 minutes
Serve: 4

Ingredients:

- 1 lb ground lamb
- 5 basil leaves, minced
- 10 mint leaves, minced
- 1/4 cup fresh parsley, chopped
- 1 tsp dried oregano
- 1 cup feta cheese, crumbled
- 1 tbsp garlic, minced
- 1 jalapeno pepper, minced
- 1/4 tsp pepper
- 1/2 tsp kosher salt

Directions:

1. Insert wire rack in rack position 6. Select bake, set temperature 390 F, timer for 8 minutes. Press start to preheat the oven.
2. Add all ingredients into the mixing bowl and mix until well combined.
3. Make four equal shape patties from meat mixture and place on a baking sheet and bake for 8 minutes.
4. Serve and enjoy.

Nutritional Value (Amount per Serving):

- Calories 330
- Fat 16.6 g
- Carbohydrates 5.4 g
- Sugar 1.7 g
- Protein 38.5 g
- Cholesterol 135 mg

Ranch Pork Chops

Preparation Time: 10 minutes
Cooking Time: 35 minutes
Serve: 4

Ingredients:

- 4 pork chops, boneless
- 4 tbsp olive oil
- 1 1/2 tbsp ranch seasoning

Directions:

1. Mix together ranch seasoning and olive oil and brush over pork chops.
2. Place pork chops in a mesh basket and bake at 400 F for 35 minutes.
3. Serve and enjoy.

Nutritional Value (Amount per Serving):

- Calories 387
- Fat 33.9 g
- Carbohydrates 0 g
- Sugar 0 g
- Protein 18 g
- Cholesterol 69 mg

Meatballs

Preparation Time: 10 minutes
Cooking Time: 20 minutes
Serve: 8

Ingredients:

- 2 lbs ground beef
- 1 1/2 cups whole wheat bread crumbs
- 12 oz jar roasted red peppers
- 1/4 cup fresh parsley, chopped
- 1/2 cup fresh basil, chopped
- 1/3 cup tomato sauce
- 2 eggs, lightly beaten
- 1/4 tsp pepper
- 1/2 tsp salt

Directions:

1. Spray a baking sheet with cooking spray and set aside.
2. Insert wire rack in rack position 6. Select bake, set temperature 350 F, timer for 20 minutes. Press start to preheat the oven.
3. Add all ingredients into the large mixing bowl and mix until well combined.
4. Make small meatballs from mixture and place on a prepared baking sheet and bake for 20 minutes.
5. Serve and enjoy.

Nutritional Value (Amount per Serving):

- Calories 304
- Fat 9.1 g
- Carbohydrates 12.6 g
- Sugar 0.5g
- Protein 38.1 g
- Cholesterol 142 mg

Lamb Patties

Preparation Time: 10 minutes
Cooking Time: 8 minutes
Serve: 4

Ingredients:

- 1 lb ground lamb
- 1 tsp dried oregano
- 1 cup feta cheese, crumbled
- 1 tbsp garlic, minced
- 1 jalapeno pepper, minced
- 5 basil leaves, minced
- 10 mint leaves, minced
- 1/4 cup fresh parsley, chopped
- 1/4 tsp pepper
- 1/2 tsp kosher salt

Directions:

1. Add all ingredients into the bowl and mix until well combined.
2. Make patties from meat mixture and place on a mesh tray and bake at 390 F for 8 minutes.
3. Serve and enjoy.

Nutritional Value (Amount per Serving):

- Calories 330
- Fat 16.6 g
- Carbohydrates 5.4 g
- Sugar 1.7 g
- Protein 38.5 g
- Cholesterol 135 mg

Rosemary Pork Chops

Preparation Time: 10 minutes
Cooking Time: 25 minutes
Serve: 4

Ingredients:

- 4 pork chops, boneless and cut 1/2-inch thick
- 2 garlic cloves, minced
- 1 tsp dried rosemary, crushed
- 1/4 tsp pepper
- 1/4 tsp salt

Directions:

1. Season pork chops with pepper and salt.
2. In a small bowl, mix together garlic and rosemary and rub all over pork chops.
3. Place pork chops on a mesh tray and bake at 350 F for 35 minutes.
4. Serve and enjoy.

Nutritional Value (Amount per Serving):

- Calories 208
- Fat 16 g
- Carbohydrates 0.6 g
- Sugar 0 g
- Protein 14.5 g
- Cholesterol 55 mg

Juicy Pork Chops

Preparation Time: 10 minutes
Cooking Time: 18 minutes
Serve: 2

Ingredients:

- 2 pork chops, boneless
- 1 tsp garlic powder
- 1 tsp onion powder
- 1/2 tbsp paprika
- 1 tbsp olive oil
- 1/2 tsp oregano
- Pepper
- Salt

Directions:

1. Coat pork chops with oil and place in a baking dish.
2. Mix oregano, garlic powder, onion powder, paprika, pepper, and salt and sprinkle over pork chops.
3. Place baking dish on a wire rack and bake in the oven at 400 F for 18 minutes.
4. Serve and enjoy.

Nutritional Value (Amount per Serving):

- Calories 331
- Fat 27.2 g
- Carbohydrates 3.2 g
- Sugar 1 g
- Protein 18.7 g
- Cholesterol 69 mg

Olive Feta Beef

Preparation Time: 10 minutes
Cooking Time: 6 hours
Serve: 6

Ingredients:

- 2 lbs beef stew meat, cut into half-inch pieces
- 1 cup olives, pitted and cut in half
- 30 oz can tomatoes, diced
- 1/2 cup feta cheese, crumbled
- 1/4 tsp pepper
- 1/2 tsp salt

Directions:

1. Insert wire rack in rack position 8. Select slow cook, Set HIGH for 6 hours. Press start to preheat the oven.
2. Add all ingredients into the dutch oven and stir well.
3. Cover the dutch oven with lid and cook on high for 6 hours.
4. Season with pepper and salt.
5. Stir well and serve.

Nutritional Value (Amount per Serving):

- Calories 370
- Fat 14.5 g
- Carbohydrates 9.2 g
- Sugar 5.3 g
- Protein 49.1 g
- Cholesterol 8 mg

Olives Artichokes Beef

Preparation Time: 10 minutes
Cooking Time: 7 hours
Serve: 6

Ingredients:

- 2 lbs stew beef, cut into 1-inch cubes
- 14 oz can artichoke hearts, drained and halved
- 1/2 cup olives, pitted and chopped
- 14 oz can tomatoes, diced
- 15 oz can tomato sauce
- 32 oz chicken stock
- 2 garlic cloves, chopped
- 1 onion, diced
- 1 tsp dried basil
- 1 tsp dried parsley
- 1 bay leaf
- 1/2 tsp ground cumin
- 1 tsp dried oregano
- 1 tbsp olive oil

Directions:

1. Insert wire rack in rack position 8. Select slow cook, Set LOW for 7 hours. Press start to preheat the oven.
2. Heat olive oil in a large pan over medium-high heat.
3. Add meat and cook until brown, about 2 minutes on each side.
4. Transfer meat into the dutch oven.
5. Pour remaining ingredients over the meat and stir well.
6. Cover and dutch oven with lid and cook on low for 7 hours.
7. Serve and enjoy.

Nutritional Value (Amount per Serving):

- Calories 322
- Fat 13.2 g
- Carbohydrates 14.2 g
- Sugar 7.1 g
- Protein 36.8 g
- Cholesterol 10 mg

Meatballs

Preparation Time: 10 minutes
Cooking Time: 20 minutes
Serve: 8

Ingredients:

- 2 lbs ground beef
- 1/2 cup fresh basil, chopped
- 1/3 cup tomato sauce
- 2 eggs, lightly beaten
- 1 1/2 cups whole wheat breadcrumbs
- 12 oz jar roasted red peppers
- 1/4 cup fresh parsley, chopped
- 1/4 tsp pepper
- 1/2 tsp salt

Directions:

1. Add all ingredients into the large mixing bowl and mix until well combined.
2. Make balls from meat mixture and place on a mesh tray and bake at 350 F for 20 minutes.
3. Serve and enjoy.

Nutritional Value (Amount per Serving):

- Calories 304
- Fat 9.1 g
- Carbohydrates 12.6 g
- Sugar 0.5g
- Protein 38.1 g
- Cholesterol 142 mg

Creamy Pork Chops

Preparation Time: 10 minutes
Cooking Time: 60 minutes
Serve: 3

Ingredients:

- 3 pork chops
- 5 oz can cream of mushrooms soup
- 1 cup breadcrumbs
- 2 tbsp flour
- 1/2 tsp garlic powder
- 1/4 cup chicken broth
- 1/2 tbsp Worcestershire sauce
- 1/4 cup milk
- 1 tsp parsley
- 1 egg, lightly beaten

Directions:

1. Spray a baking dish with cooking spray and set aside.
2. Add egg in a shallow dish.
3. In a bowl mix together flour and seasoning.
4. Add breadcrumbs to a plate.
5. Coat pork chops with flour then dip in egg and coat with breadcrumbs and place in baking dish.
6. Place baking dish on a wire rack and bake in the oven at 350 F for 35 minutes.
7. Mix broth, Worcestershire sauce, milk, and soup and pour over pork chops and bake for 25 minutes more.
8. Serve and enjoy.

Nutritional Value (Amount per Serving):

- Calories 480
- Fat 24.6 g

- Carbohydrates 35.8 g
- Sugar 5 g
- Protein 26.9 g
- Cholesterol 126 mg

Tasty Parmesan Pork Chops

Preparation Time: 10 minutes
Cooking Time: 35 minutes
Serve: 4

Ingredients:

- 2 pork chops, boneless
- 1/8 tsp paprika
- 2 tbsp breadcrumbs
- 1/3 cup parmesan cheese, grated
- 1 tbsp olive oil
- 1/4 tsp garlic powder
- 1/2 tsp dried parsley
- Pepper
- Salt

Directions:

1. Spray a baking dish with cooking spray and set aside.
2. Coat pork chops with olive oil.
3. In a shallow dish, mix breadcrumbs, cheese, paprika, parsley, garlic powder, pepper, and salt.
4. Coat pork chops with breadcrumb mixture and place in baking dish.
5. Place baking dish on a wire rack and bake in the oven at 350 F for 35 minutes.
6. Serve and enjoy.

Nutritional Value (Amount per Serving):

- Calories 200
- Fat 15.5 g
- Carbohydrates 2.9 g
- Sugar 0.3 g
- Protein 12.3 g
- Cholesterol 41 mg

Garlic Butter Pork Chops

Preparation Time: 10 minutes
Cooking Time: 15 minutes
Serve: 2

Ingredients:

- 2 pork chops
- 4 tbsp butter, melted
- 2 garlic cloves, minced
- 1 tbsp thyme, chopped
- Pepper
- Salt

Directions:

1. Spray a baking dish with cooking spray and set aside.
2. Season pork chops with pepper and salt and place in a baking dish.
3. Mix butter, thyme, and garlic and pour over pork chops.
4. Place baking dish on a wire rack and bake at 375 F for 15 minutes.
5. Serve and enjoy.

Nutritional Value (Amount per Serving):

- Calories 468
- Fat 43 g
- Carbohydrates 1.9 g
- Sugar 0.1 g
- Protein 18.5 g
- Cholesterol 130 mg

Italian Beef Roast

Preparation Time: 10 minutes
Cooking Time: 6 hours
Serve: 6

Ingredients:

- 2 lbs chuck roast, boneless
- 1/4 cup fresh parsley, chopped
- 1/4 cup olives, chopped
- 1/2 cup chicken stock
- 2 tbsp vinegar
- 2 tsp herb de Provence
- 1/3 cup sun-dried tomatoes, chopped
- 1 tbsp garlic, chopped

Directions:

1. Insert wire rack in rack position 8. Select slow cook, Set HIGH for 6 hours. Press start to preheat the oven.
2. Add all ingredients into the dutch oven and stir well.
3. Cover the dutch oven with lid and cook on high for 6 hours.
4. Shred meat using a fork.
5. Stir and serve.

Nutritional Value (Amount per Serving):

- Calories 345
- Fat 13 g
- Carbohydrates 2.3 g
- Sugar 0.5 g
- Protein 50 g
- Cholesterol 153 mg

Pork Tenderloin

Preparation Time: 10 minutes
Cooking Time: 35 minutes
Serve: 3

Ingredients:

- 1 lb pork tenderloin
- 1/2 tbsp dried rosemary
- 1 tbsp olive oil
- Pepper
- Salt

Directions:

1. Mix rosemary and olive oil and rub over pork tenderloin.
2. Place pork tenderloin in baking dish.
3. Place baking dish on a wire rack and bake at 400 F for 35 minutes.
4. Remove from oven and season with pepper and salt.
5. Slice and serve.

Nutritional Value (Amount per Serving):

- Calories 258
- Fat 10.1 g
- Carbohydrates 0.4 g
- Sugar 0 g
- Protein 39.6 g
- Cholesterol 110 mg

Mediterranean Beef

Preparation Time: 10 minutes
Cooking Time: 8 hours
Serve: 8

Ingredients:

- 3 lbs beef pot roast, cut into small pieces
- 1/2 tsp ground cinnamon
- 1/2 tsp turmeric powder
- 1 tsp garlic, minced
- 15 oz frozen mixed vegetables
- 1/2 tsp ground ginger
- 1 tbsp beef bouillon granules
- 1 1/2 tbsp garam masala
- 2 cups of water
- 1 tsp salt

Directions:

1. Insert wire rack in rack position 8. Select slow cook, Set LOW for 8 hours. Press start to preheat the oven.
2. Add all ingredients into the dutch oven and stir everything well.
3. Cover the dutch oven with lid and cook on low for 8 hours.
4. Stir well and serve.

Nutritional Value (Amount per Serving):

- Calories 157
- Fat 3.2 g
- Carbohydrates 19.5 g
- Sugar 5.8 g
- Protein 13 g
- Cholesterol 17 mg

Meatballs

Preparation Time: 10 minutes
Cooking Time: 20 minutes
Serve: 6

Ingredients:

- 2 lbs ground beef
- 1 egg, lightly beaten
- 1 tsp oregano
- 1 tsp cinnamon
- 2 tsp cumin
- 2 tsp coriander
- 1 tsp garlic, minced
- 1 small onion, grated
- 1 tbsp fresh mint, chopped
- 1/4 cup fresh parsley, minced
- 1/2 tsp allspice
- 1 tsp paprika
- Pepper
- Salt

Directions:

1. Insert wire rack in rack position 6. Select bake, set temperature 390 F, timer for 20 minutes. Press start to preheat the oven.
2. Add all ingredients into the large mixing bowl and mix until well combined.
3. Make small balls from the meat mixture and place them on a baking sheet and bake for 20 minutes.
4. Serve and enjoy.

Nutritional Value (Amount per Serving):

- Calories 304
- Fat 10.4 g

- Carbohydrates 2.7 g
- Sugar 10.7 g
- Protein 47.3 g
- Cholesterol 162 mg

Baked Beef Casserole

Preparation Time: 10 minutes
Cooking Time: 1 hour 30 minutes
Serve: 6

Ingredients:

- 1 lb lean stew beef, cut into chunks
- 1/4 tsp garlic powder
- 1 tbsp tomato puree
- 2 cups beef stock
- 2 tbsp olive oil
- 2 tsp herb de Provence
- 3 tsp paprika
- 4 oz black olives, sliced
- 7 oz can tomatoes, chopped

Directions:

1. Insert wire rack in rack position 6. Select bake, set temperature 350 F, timer for 1 hour 30 minutes. Press start to preheat the oven.
2. Heat oil in a pan over medium heat. Add meat to the pan and cook until brown.
3. Add stock, olives, tomatoes, tomato puree, garlic powder, herb de Provence, and paprika. Stir well and bring to boil.
4. Transfer meat mixture into the casserole dish.
5. Cover dish with foil and cook in the oven for 1 hour 30 minutes.
6. Serve and enjoy.

Nutritional Value (Amount per Serving):

- Calories 228
- Fat 11.6 g
- Carbohydrates 5.8g
- Sugar 1.4 g
- Protein 26 g

- Cholesterol 11 mg

Chapter 4: Fish & Seafood

Dijon Salmon

Preparation Time: 10 minutes
Cooking Time: 12 minutes
Serve: 4

Ingredients:

- 4 salmon fillets
- 2 tbsp ground Dijon mustard
- 3 tbsp maple syrup

Directions:

1. Arrange salmon fillets on a mesh tray.
2. Mix together Dijon mustard and maple syrup and brush over salmon fillets.
3. Bake salmon fillets at 390 F for 12 minutes.
4. Serve and enjoy.

Nutritional Value (Amount per Serving):

- Calories 282
- Fat 11 g
- Carbohydrates 10.1 g
- Sugar 8.9 g
- Protein 34.5 g
- Cholesterol 78 mg

Tasty Cajun Shrimp

Preparation Time: 10 minutes
Cooking Time: 10 minutes
Serve: 4

Ingredients:

- 1 lb shrimp, deveined & peeled
- 2 tbsp olive oil
- 3/4 tbsp Cajun seasoning

Directions:

1. Spray a baking dish with cooking spray and set aside.
2. Add shrimp, Cajun seasoning, and oil into the bowl and toss well.
3. Add shrimp into the baking dish.
4. Place baking dish on a wire rack and bake at 350 F for 10 minutes.
5. Serve and enjoy.

Nutritional Value (Amount per Serving):

- Calories 195
- Fat 8.9 g
- Carbohydrates 1.7 g
- Sugar 0 g
- Protein 25.9 g
- Cholesterol 239 mg

Baked Lemon Butter Cod

Preparation Time: 10 minutes
Cooking Time: 20 minutes
Serve: 4

Ingredients:

- 1 1/2 lb cod fillet
- 4 garlic cloves, minced
- 2 lemon juice
- 2 tbsp olive oil
- 1 lemon, sliced
- 1/4 cup butter, diced
- Pepper
- Salt

Directions:

1. Place codpieces in the baking dish and season with pepper and salt.
2. Whisk together garlic, lemon juice, and olive oil and pour over cod.
3. Arrange butter pieces and lemon slices on top of cod.
4. Place baking dish on a wire rack and bake at 390 F for 20 minutes.
5. Serve and enjoy.

Nutritional Value (Amount per Serving):

- Calories 309
- Fat 20.3 g
- Carbohydrates 1.7 g
- Sugar 0.6 g
- Protein 30.9 g
- Cholesterol 114 mg

Scallop Gratin

Preparation Time: 10 minutes
Cooking Time: 8 minutes
Serve: 4

Ingredients:

- 1 1/2 lbs sea scallops
- 1 lemon juice
- 1/4 cup white wine
- 1/4 cup cream cheese, softened
- 1/4 cup parmesan cheese, shaved
- 1 tbsp tarragon, chopped
- Pepper
- Salt

Directions:

1. Add scallops to the baking dish.
2. In a bowl, whisk together lemon juice, cream cheese, white wine, tarragon, parmesan cheese, pepper, and salt and pour over scallops.
3. Place baking dish on a wire rack and bake at 390 F for 8 minutes.
4. Serve and enjoy.

Nutritional Value (Amount per Serving):

- Calories 235
- Fat 7.7 g
- Carbohydrates 5.5 g
- Sugar 0.4 g
- Protein 31.6 g
- Cholesterol 76 mg

Greek Scallops

Preparation Time: 10 minutes
Cooking Time: 15 minutes
Serve: 4

Ingredients:

- 1 1/2 lbs sea scallops
- 4 sun-dried tomatoes, minced
- 2 tbsp olives, chopped
- 8 tbsp butter, melted
- 2 garlic cloves, minced
- 1 tbsp dried basil
- Pepper
- Salt

Directions:

1. Spray a baking dish with cooking spray and set aside.
2. Add all ingredients into the mixing bowl and toss well.
3. Pour scallops mixture into the baking dish.
4. Place baking dish on a wire rack and bake at 400 F for 15 minutes.
5. Serve and enjoy.

Nutritional Value (Amount per Serving):

- Calories 390
- Fat 25.8 g
- Carbohydrates 9.9 g
- Sugar 3.3 g
- Protein 30 g
- Cholesterol 117 mg

Garlic Tomato Shrimp

Preparation Time: 10 minutes
Cooking Time: 25 minutes
Serve: 4

Ingredients:

- 1 lb shrimp, peeled
- 2 cups grape tomatoes
- 1 tbsp olive oil
- 1 tbsp garlic, sliced
- Pepper
- Salt

Directions:

1. Spray a baking dish with cooking spray and set aside.
2. Add shrimp, oil, garlic, grape tomatoes, pepper, and salt into the mixing bowl and toss well.
3. Transfer shrimp mixture into the baking dish.
4. Place baking dish on a wire rack and bake at 400 F for 25 minutes.
5. Serve and enjoy.

Nutritional Value (Amount per Serving):

- Calories 184
- Fat 5.6 g
- Carbohydrates 5.9 g
- Sugar 2.4 g
- Protein 26.8 g
- Cholesterol 239 mg

Rosemary Shrimp

Preparation Time: 10 minutes
Cooking Time: 10 minutes
Serve: 4

Ingredients:

- 1 lb shrimp, peeled and deveined
- 1/2 tbsp fresh rosemary, chopped
- 1 garlic clove, minced
- 1 tbsp olive oil
- Pepper
- Salt

Directions:

1. Spray a baking dish with cooking spray and set aside.
2. Add shrimp, rosemary, garlic, oil, pepper, and salt in a mixing bowl and toss well.
3. Pour shrimp mixture into the baking dish.
4. Place baking dish on a wire rack and bake at 400 F for 10 minutes.
5. Serve and enjoy.

Nutritional Value (Amount per Serving):

- Calories 167
- Fat 5.5 g
- Carbohydrates 2.3 g
- Sugar 0 g
- Protein 25.9 g
- Cholesterol 239 mg

Shrimp Casserole

Preparation Time: 10 minutes
Cooking Time: 12 minutes
Serve: 4

Ingredients:

- 1 lb shrimp, peeled and deveined
- 1/4 cup butter, melted
- 2 tbsp white wine
- 1 tbsp garlic, minced
- 2 tbsp fresh parsley, chopped
- 1/2 cup breadcrumbs
- Pepper
- Salt

Directions:

1. Spray a baking dish with cooking spray and set aside.
2. Add shrimp into the mixing bowl. Pour remaining ingredients over shrimp and toss well.
3. Pour shrimp mixture into the baking dish.
4. Place baking dish on a wire rack and bake at 400 F for 12 minutes.
5. Serve and enjoy.

Nutritional Value (Amount per Serving):

- Calories 300
- Fat 14.2 g
- Carbohydrates 12.5 g
- Sugar 1 g
- Protein 28 g
- Cholesterol 269 mg

Spicy Shrimp

Preparation Time: 10 minutes
Cooking Time: 8 minutes
Serve: 4

Ingredients:

- 1 lb shrimp, peeled and deveined
- 1 tbsp soy sauce
- 3 tbsp butter, melted
- 1 tsp garlic, chopped
- 1 tbsp chili paste

Directions:

1. Spray a baking dish with cooking spray and set aside.
2. Add shrimp into the baking dish.
3. In a bowl, mix together butter, soy sauce, chili paste, and garlic and pour over shrimp and mix well.
4. Place baking dish on a wire rack and bake at 400 F for 8 minutes.
5. Serve and enjoy.

Nutritional Value (Amount per Serving):

- Calories 227
- Fat 11.2 g
- Carbohydrates 3.8 g
- Sugar 1.1 g
- Protein 26.5 g
- Cholesterol 263 mg

Spicy Salmon

Preparation Time: 10 minutes
Cooking Time: 12 minutes
Serve:

Ingredients:

- 4 salmon fillets
- 2 tsp Cajun seasoning
- 4 tbsp brown sugar
- Salt

Directions:

1. Mix together Cajun seasoning, brown sugar, and salt and rub all over salmon.
2. Place salmon on a mesh tray and bake at 390 F for 12 minutes.
3. Serve and enjoy.

Nutritional Value (Amount per Serving):

- Calories 270
- Fat 11 g
- Carbohydrates 8.8 g
- Sugar 8.7 g
- Protein 34.6 g
- Cholesterol 78 mg

Chapter 5: Vegetable & Side Dishes

Baked Zucchini

Preparation Time: 10 minutes
Cooking Time: 40 minutes
Serve: 8

Ingredients:

- 4 cups zucchini, sliced
- 1 tbsp butter, melted
- 4 eggs, lightly beaten
- 2 cups crushed crackers
- 1 1/2 cup milk
- 2 cups cheddar cheese, shredded

Directions:

1. Spray 9*13-inch casserole dish with cooking spray and set aside.
2. Add sliced zucchini into the casserole dish.
3. In a bowl, whisk together eggs, butter, milk, and 1 cup cheese and pour over sliced zucchini.
4. Sprinkle with crushed crackers and remaining cheese.
5. Place casserole dish on a wire rack and bake at 350 F for 40 minutes.
6. Serve and enjoy.

Nutritional Value (Amount per Serving):

- Calories 251
- Fat 18.8 g
- Carbohydrates 8.7 g
- Sugar 4.1 g
- Protein 12.5 g
- Cholesterol 115 mg

Baked Frozen Vegetables

Preparation Time: 10 minutes
Cooking Time: 30 minutes
Serve: 3

Ingredients:

- 12 oz mixed frozen vegetables
- 1/2 tsp onion powder
- 1/2 tsp garlic powder
- 2 tbsp olive oil
- 1/2 tsp pepper
- 1/2 tsp salt

Directions:

1. In a bowl, toss frozen mixed vegetables with remaining ingredients.
2. Spread vegetables on a mesh tray and bake at 390 F for 30 minutes.
3. Serve and enjoy.

Nutritional Value (Amount per Serving):

- Calories 158
- Fat 9.5 g
- Carbohydrates 15.7 g
- Sugar 3.8 g
- Protein 3.4 g
- Cholesterol 0 mg

Baked Root Vegetables

Preparation Time: 10 minutes
Cooking Time: 30 minutes
Serve: 4

Ingredients:

- 1 onion, cut into wedges
- 3 medium carrots, cut into 1-inch pieces
- 2 tsp Italian seasoning
- 1 tbsp olive oil
- 1 rutabaga, peeled and cut into 1-inch chunks
- 1 parsnip, cut into 1-inch chunks
- 2 tbsp balsamic vinegar
- Pepper
- Salt

Directions:

1. In a bowl, toss vegetables with remaining ingredients and spread on a mesh tray, and bake at 390 F for 30 minutes.
2. Serve and enjoy.

Nutritional Value (Amount per Serving):

- Calories 128
- Fat 4.5 g
- Carbohydrates 21.3 g
- Sugar 10.7 g
- Protein 2.3 g
- Cholesterol 2 mg

Lemon Baked Potatoes

Preparation Time: 10 minutes
Cooking Time: 60 minutes
Serve: 4

Ingredients:

- 5 potatoes, cut into wedges
- 1/2 cup lemon juice
- 1/3 cup olive oil
- 2 tsp dried oregano
- 3 garlic cloves, minced
- 1 cup of water
- Pepper
- Salt

Directions:

1. Add potato wedges into the 9*13-inch baking dish.
2. In a bowl, whisk together oregano, garlic, lemon juice, oil, water, pepper, and salt, and pour over potatoes.
3. Place baking dish on a wire rack and bake at 325 F for 60 minutes.
4. Serve and enjoy.

Nutritional Value (Amount per Serving):

- Calories 341
- Fat 17.4 g
- Carbohydrates 43.7 g
- Sugar 3.8 g
- Protein 4.9 g
- Cholesterol 43.7 mg

Baked Butternut Squash

Preparation Time: 10 minutes
Cooking Time: 40 minutes
Serve: 4

Ingredients:

- 3 lbs butternut squash, peeled, seeded, and cut into 1-inch cubes
- 1 1/2 tbsp maple syrup
- 1 1/2 tbsp olive oil
- 1/2 tsp cinnamon
- Pepper
- Salt

Directions:

1. In a mixing bowl, toss squash cubes with the remaining ingredients.
2. Spread squash cubes on a mesh tray and bake at 400 F for 40 minutes.
3. Serve and enjoy.

Nutritional Value (Amount per Serving):

- Calories 219
- Fat 5.6 g
- Carbohydrates 45.1 g
- Sugar 12 g
- Protein 3.4 g
- Cholesterol 0 mg

Potato Casserole

Preparation Time: 10 minutes
Cooking Time: 60 minutes
Serve: 6

Ingredients:

- 2 eggs
- 8 oz cream cheese, softened
- 1 cup cheddar cheese, shredded
- 10 potatoes, peeled and halved
- 3 tbsp butter
- 1 cup sour cream
- Pepper
- Salt

Directions:

1. Add potatoes to the boiling water and boil for 10 minutes or until tender. Drain well and place in a mixing bowl.
2. Mash the potatoes using masher until smooth.
3. Add remaining ingredients into the mashed potatoes and stir well to combine.
4. Pour potato mixture into the casserole dish
5. Place casserole dish on a wire rack and bake at 325 F for 50 minutes.
6. Serve and enjoy.

Nutritional Value (Amount per Serving):

- Calories 607
- Fat 35 g
- Carbohydrates 58.8 g
- Sugar 4.4 g
- Protein 16.6 g
- Cholesterol 148 mg

Zucchini Tomato Bake

Preparation Time: 10 minutes
Cooking Time: 30 minutes
Serve: 6

Ingredients:

- 3 tomatoes, sliced
- 2 yellow squash, sliced
- 2 medium zucchinis, sliced
- 3/4 cup parmesan cheese, shredded
- 1 tbsp olive oil
- Pepper
- Salt

Directions:

1. Spray a 9*13-inch baking dish with cooking spray and set aside.
2. Arrange sliced tomatoes, squash, and zucchinis alternately in the baking dish. Drizzle with olive oil and season with pepper and salt.
3. Sprinkle parmesan cheese on top of vegetables.
4. Place baking dish on a wire rack and bake at 350 F for 30 minutes.
5. Serve and enjoy.

Nutritional Value (Amount per Serving):

- Calories 80
- Fat 5 g
- Carbohydrates 5.5 g
- Sugar 3.1 g
- Protein 4.9 g
- Cholesterol 8 mg

Baked Carrots

Preparation Time: 10 minutes
Cooking Time: 30 minutes
Serve: 4

Ingredients:

- 24 baby carrots
- 1/4 cup brown sugar
- 1 tsp cinnamon
- 6 tbsp butter, melted
- Pepper
- Salt

Directions:

1. Arrange baby carrots in the baking dish.
2. Pour melted butter over baby carrots.
3. Sprinkle cinnamon, brown sugar, pepper, and salt over baby carrots.
4. Place baking dish on a wire rack and bake at 390 F for 30 minutes.
5. Serve and enjoy.

Nutritional Value (Amount per Serving):

- Calories 210
- Fat 17.4 g
- Carbohydrates 14.3 g
- Sugar 11.7 g
- Protein 0.6 g
- Cholesterol 46 mg

Baked Sweet Potatoes

Preparation Time: 10 minutes
Cooking Time: 40 minutes
Serve: 4

Ingredients:

- 2 large sweet potatoes, cut into 1-inch cubes
- 1/2 tsp chili powder
- 3/4 tsp paprika
- 1 tbsp olive oil
- 1/4 tsp onion powder
- 1/2 tsp garlic powder
- 1/2 tsp cumin
- 1/4 tsp pepper
- 1/2 tsp salt

Directions:

1. In a bowl, toss sweet potatoes with remaining ingredients until well coated.
2. Spread sweet potatoes on a mesh tray and bake at 390 F for 40 minutes.
3. Serve and enjoy.

Nutritional Value (Amount per Serving):

- Calories 94
- Fat 3.8 g
- Carbohydrates 14.9 g
- Sugar 0.5 g
- Protein 1 g
- Cholesterol 0 mg

Delicious Paprika Zucchini

Preparation Time: 10 minutes
Cooking Time: 20 minutes
Serve: 2

Ingredients:

- 3 medium zucchinis, cut into chunks
- 1 tsp garlic powder
- 2 tbsp olive oil
- 1 tsp paprika
- Pepper
- Salt

Directions:

1. In a mixing bowl, toss zucchini chunks with paprika, garlic powder, oil, pepper, and salt.
2. Spread zucchini on a mesh tray and bake at 390 F for 15-20 minutes.
3. Serve and enjoy.

Nutritional Value (Amount per Serving):

- Calories 131
- Fat 14.2 g
- Carbohydrates 2.2 g
- Sugar 0.5 g
- Protein 0.9 g
- Cholesterol 0 mg

Chapter 6: Snacks & Appetizers

Spicy Cheese Dip

Preparation Time: 10 minutes
Cooking Time: 30 minutes
Serve: 10

Ingredients:

- 16 oz cream cheese, softened
- 1/2 cup hot salsa
- 3 cups cheddar cheese, shredded
- 1 cup sour cream

Directions:

1. Spray an 8*8-inch baking dish with cooking spray and set aside.
2. In a mixing bowl, mix together all ingredients until well combined and pour into the baking dish.
3. Place baking dish on a wire rack and bake in the oven at 350 F for 25 minutes.
4. Serve and enjoy.

Nutritional Value (Amount per Serving):

- Calories 348
- Fat 31.9 g
- Carbohydrates 3.4 g
- Sugar 0.7 g
- Protein 12.8 g
- Cholesterol 96 mg

Tasty Sweet Potato Fries

Preparation Time: 10 minutes
Cooking Time: 16 minutes
Serve: 2

Ingredients:

- 2 sweet potatoes, peeled and cut into fries shape
- 1/4 tsp chili powder
- 1 tbsp olive oil
- Salt

Directions:

1. In a mixing bowl, add sweet potato fries, chili powder, garlic powder, olive oil, and salt and toss until well coated.
2. Arrange sweet potato fries on a mesh tray and bake at 380 F for 16 minutes.
3. Serve and enjoy.

Nutritional Value (Amount per Serving):

- Calories 238
- Fat 7.3 g
- Carbohydrates 42 g
- Sugar 0.8 g
- Protein 2.3 g
- Cholesterol 0 mg

Goat Cheese Dip

Preparation Time: 10 minutes
Cooking Time: 20 minutes
Serve: 8

Ingredients:

- 12 oz goat cheese
- 4 garlic cloves, minced
- 2 tbsp olive oil
- 1/2 cup parmesan cheese, shredded
- 2 tsp rosemary, chopped
- 1 tsp red pepper flakes
- 4 oz cream cheese
- 1/2 tsp salt

Directions:

1. Spray a baking dish with cooking spray and set aside.
2. Add all ingredients into the mixing bowl and mix until well combined.
3. Pour mixture into the baking dish.
4. Place baking dish on a wire rack and bake in the oven at 390 F for 20 minutes.
5. Serve and enjoy.

Nutritional Value (Amount per Serving):

- Calories 294
- Fat 24.9 g
- Carbohydrates 2.3 g
- Sugar 1 g
- Protein 16 g
- Cholesterol 64 mg

Parmesan Potatoes

Preparation Time: 10 minutes
Cooking Time: 45 minutes
Serve: 4

Ingredients:

- 5 potatoes, cut into wedges
- 2 tbsp lemon juice
- 1/3 cup olive oil
- 2 thyme sprigs
- 1/2 cup parmesan cheese, grated
- 2 garlic cloves, minced
- Pepper
- Salt

Directions:

1. Spray a 9*13-inch baking dish with cooking spray and set aside.
2. Add potato wedges into the baking dish.
3. Mix together lemon juice, oil, garlic, thyme, cheese, pepper, and salt and pour over potatoes and toss well.
4. Place baking dish on a wire rack and bake in the oven at 325 F for 45 minutes.
5. Serve and enjoy.

Nutritional Value (Amount per Serving):

- Calories 374
- Fat 19.7 g
- Carbohydrates 44.3 g
- Sugar 3.3 g
- Protein 8.5 g
- Cholesterol 8 mg

Sweet Chickpeas

Preparation Time: 10 minutes
Cooking Time: 12 minutes
Serve: 4

Ingredients:

- 14 oz can chickpeas, rinsed, drained and pat dry
- 1 tbsp olive oil
- 1/2 tsp ground cinnamon
- 1 tbsp maple syrup
- Pepper
- Salt

Directions:

1. Spread chickpeas on a mesh tray and bake at 390 F for 12 minutes.
2. In a large bowl, mix together cinnamon, maple syrup, oil, pepper, and salt. Add chickpeas and toss well.
3. Serve and enjoy.

Nutritional Value (Amount per Serving):

- Calories 170
- Fat 4.7 g
- Carbohydrates 27.6 g
- Sugar 3 g
- Protein 5.3 g
- Cholesterol 0 mg

Parmesan Carrot Fries

Preparation Time: 10 minutes
Cooking Time: 15 minutes
Serve: 4

Ingredients:

- 4 carrots, peeled and cut into fries
- 2 tbsp parmesan cheese, grated
- 1 1/2 tbsp garlic, minced
- 2 tbsp olive oil
- Pepper
- Salt

Directions:

1. Add carrots and remaining ingredients into the mixing bowl and toss well.
2. Add carrots fries on a mesh tray and bake at 350 F for 15 minutes.
3. Serve and enjoy.

Nutritional Value (Amount per Serving):

- Calories 99
- Fat 7.6 g
- Carbohydrates 7.2 g
- Sugar 3 g
- Protein 1.6 g
- Cholesterol 2 mg

Flavorful Ranch Potatoes

Preparation Time: 10 minutes
Cooking Time: 20 minutes
Serve: 2

Ingredients:

- 1/2 lb baby potatoes, wash and cut in half
- 1/2 tbsp olive oil
- 1/4 tsp dill
- 1/4 tsp chives
- 1/4 tsp paprika
- 1/4 tsp onion powder
- 1/4 tsp garlic powder
- 1/4 tsp parsley
- Salt

Directions:

1. Add all ingredients into the mixing bowl and toss well.
2. Spread potatoes on a mesh tray and bake at 400 F for 20 minutes.
3. Serve and enjoy.

Nutritional Value (Amount per Serving):

- Calories 99
- Fat 3.7 g
- Carbohydrates 14.8 g
- Sugar 0.2 g
- Protein 3.1 g
- Cholesterol 0 mg

Tasty Broccoli Nuggets

Preparation Time: 10 minutes
Cooking Time: 20 minutes
Serve: 4

Ingredients:

- 1/4 cup almond flour
- 1 cup cheddar cheese, shredded
- 2 cups broccoli florets, cooked until soften
- 2 egg whites
- 1/8 tsp salt

Directions:

1. Add cooked broccoli to the bowl and using masher mash broccoli into small pieces.
2. Add remaining ingredients to the bowl and mix until well combined.
3. Drop 20 scoops of broccoli mixture onto the mesh tray and bake at 350 F for 20 minutes.
4. Serve and enjoy.

Nutritional Value (Amount per Serving):

- Calories 180
- Fat 12.9 g
- Carbohydrates 5 g
- Sugar 1 g
- Protein 11.6 g
- Cholesterol 30 mg

Chicken Dip

Preparation Time: 10 minutes
Cooking Time: 25 minutes
Serve: 8

Ingredients:

- 2 chicken breasts, skinless, boneless, cooked and shredded
- 1 cup Monterey jack cheese, shredded
- 1 cup cheddar cheese, shredded
- 1/4 cup blue cheese, crumbled
- 1/2 cup ranch dressing
- 1/2 cup buffalo wing sauce
- 8 oz cream cheese, softened

Directions:

1. Spray a 1.5-quart casserole dish with cooking spray and set aside.
2. Add cream cheese into the casserole dish and top with shredded chicken, ranch dressing, and buffalo sauce.
3. Sprinkle cheddar cheese, Monterey jack cheese, and blue cheese on top of chicken mixture.
4. Place casserole dish on a wire rack and bake in the oven at 350 F for 25 minutes.
5. Serve and enjoy.

Nutritional Value (Amount per Serving):

- Calories 298
- Fat 22.8 g
- Carbohydrates 2 g
- Sugar 0.6 g
- Protein 20.8 g
- Cholesterol 94 mg

Crab Dip

Preparation Time: 10 minutes
Cooking Time: 15 minutes
Serve: 4

Ingredients:

- 8 oz crab meat
- 1/4 cup onion, chopped
- 1 1/2 tsp garlic, minced
- 1 cup cheddar cheese, shredded
- 1/4 tsp paprika
- 1/2 tsp garlic powder
- 1/2 cup sour cream
- 1/4 cup mayonnaise
- 8 oz cream cheese, softened
- Pepper
- Salt

Directions:

1. Spray a baking dish with cooking spray and set aside.
2. Add all ingredients into the bowl and mix until well combined.
3. Pour mixture into the baking dish.
4. Place baking dish on a wire rack and bake in the oven at 390 F for 15 minutes.
5. Serve and enjoy.

Nutritional Value (Amount per Serving):

- Calories 487
- Fat 41.1 g
- Carbohydrates 9 g
- Sugar 1.7 g
- Protein 19.7 g
- Cholesterol 139 mg

Chapter 7: Dehydrate

Eggplant Chips

Preparation Time: 10 minutes
Cooking Time: 4 hours
Serve: 4

Ingredients:

- 1 eggplant, cut into 1/4-inch thick slices
- 1 tsp paprika

Directions:

1. Arrange eggplant slices on the mesh trays and sprinkle with paprika and insert in the oven.
2. Cook on DEHYDRATE mode at 145 F for 4 hours.

Nutritional Value (Amount per Serving):

- Calories 30
- Fat 0.3 g
- Carbohydrates 7 g
- Sugar 3.5 g
- Protein 1.2 g
- Cholesterol 0 mg

Cinnamon Apple Slices

Preparation Time: 10 minutes
Cooking Time: 8 hours
Serve: 4

Ingredients:

- 2 apples, cut into 1/8-inch thick slices
- 1 tsp ground cinnamon

Directions:

1. Arrange apple slices on the mesh trays and sprinkle with cinnamon and insert in the oven.
2. Cook on DEHYDRATE mode at 135 F for 8 hours.

Nutritional Value (Amount per Serving):

- Calories 59
- Fat 0.2 g
- Carbohydrates 15.9 g
- Sugar 11.6 g
- Protein 0.3 g
- Cholesterol 0 mg

Beet Chips

Preparation Time: 10 minutes
Cooking Time: 8 hours
Serve: 4

Ingredients:

- 4 medium beets, peel and sliced

Directions:

1. Arrange beet slices on the mesh trays and insert them in the oven.
2. Cook on DEHYDRATE mode at 135 F for 8 hours.

Nutritional Value (Amount per Serving):

- Calories 44
- Fat 0.2 g
- Carbohydrates 10 g
- Sugar 8 g
- Protein 1.7 g
- Cholesterol 0 mg

Parsnips Chips

Preparation Time: 10 minutes
Cooking Time: 6 hours
Serve: 2

Ingredients:

- 1 parsnip, cut into 1/4-inch thick slices

Directions:

1. Arrange parsnip slices on the mesh trays and insert them in the oven.
2. Cook on DEHYDRATE mode at 125 F for 6 hours.
3. Store parsnip chips in an airtight container.

Nutritional Value (Amount per Serving):

- Calories 50
- Fat 0.2 g
- Carbohydrates 12 g
- Sugar 3.2 g
- Protein 0.8 g
- Cholesterol 0 mg

Banana Slices

Preparation Time: 10 minutes
Cooking Time: 6 hours
Serve: 2

Ingredients:

- 2 bananas, peel & cut into 1/8-inch thick slices

Directions:

1. Arrange banana slices on the mesh trays and insert them in the oven.
2. Cook on DEHYDRATE mode at 135 F for 6 hours.

Nutritional Value (Amount per Serving):

- Calories 105
- Fat 0.4 g
- Carbohydrates 27 g
- Sugar 14.4 g
- Protein 1.3 g
- Cholesterol 0 mg

Pear Slices

Preparation Time: 10 minutes
Cooking Time: 5 hours
Serve: 4

Ingredients:

- 2 pears, cut into 1/4-inch thick slices

Directions:

1. Arrange pear slices on the mesh trays and insert them in the oven.
2. Cook on DEHYDRATE mode at 160 F for 5 hours.

Nutritional Value (Amount per Serving):

- Calories 60
- Fat 0.2 g
- Carbohydrates 15.9 g
- Sugar 10.2 g
- Protein 0.4 g
- Cholesterol 0 mg

Lemon Slices

Preparation Time: 10 minutes
Cooking Time: 10 hours
Serve: 4

Ingredients:

- 4 lemons, wash and cut into 1/4-inch thick slices

Directions:

1. Arrange lemon slices on the mesh trays and insert them in the oven.
2. Cook on DEHYDRATE mode at 125 F for 10 hours.

Nutritional Value (Amount per Serving):

- Calories 17
- Fat 0.2 g
- Carbohydrates 5.4 g
- Sugar 1.5 g
- Protein 0.6 g
- Cholesterol 0 mg

Zucchini Chips

Preparation Time: 10 minutes
Cooking Time: 8 hours
Serve: 4

Ingredients:

- 2 zucchini, cut into 1/4-inch thick slices
- 1 tsp olive oil
- Pepper
- Salt

Directions:

1. Toss zucchini slices with oil, pepper, and salt in a bowl.
2. Arrange zucchini slices on the mesh trays and insert them in the oven.
3. Cook on DEHYDRATE mode at 135 F for 8 hours.

Nutritional Value (Amount per Serving):

- Calories 26
- Fat 1.4 g
- Carbohydrates 3.3 g
- Sugar 1.7 g
- Protein 1.2 g
- Cholesterol 0 mg

Cucumber Chips

Preparation Time: 10 minutes
Cooking Time: 6 hours
Serve: 4

Ingredients:

- 1 large cucumber, sliced
- 1/8 tsp pepper
- 1/4 tsp salt

Directions:

1. Arrange cucumber slices on the mesh trays and season with pepper and salt and insert in the oven.
2. Cook on DEHYDRATE mode at 135 F for 6 hours.

Nutritional Value (Amount per Serving):

- Calories 11
- Fat 0.1 g
- Carbohydrates 2.8 g
- Sugar 1.3 g
- Protein 0.5 g
- Cholesterol 0 mg

Green Apple Slices

Preparation Time: 10 minutes
Cooking Time: 8 hours
Serve: 4

Ingredients:

- 2 green apple, cored and cut into 1/8-inch thick slices

Directions:

1. Arrange green apple slices on the mesh trays and insert them in the oven.
2. Cook on DEHYDRATE mode at 145 F for 8 hours.

Nutritional Value (Amount per Serving):

- Calories 59
- Fat 0.2 g
- Carbohydrates 15.9 g
- Sugar 11.6 g
- Protein 0.3 g
- Cholesterol 0 mg

Chapter 8: Desserts

Blueberry Muffins

Preparation Time: 10 minutes
Cooking Time: 20 minutes
Serve: 12

Ingredients:

- 3 large eggs
- 2 1/2 cups almond flour
- 3/4 cup blueberries
- 1/3 cup coconut oil, melted
- 1 1/2 tsp baking powder
- 1/2 cup erythritol
- 1/2 tsp vanilla
- 1/3 cup almond milk

Directions:

1. In a large bowl, mix together almond flour, baking powder, erythritol.
2. Stir in the coconut oil, vanilla, eggs, and almond milk.
3. Add blueberries and fold well.
4. Pour batter into the silicone muffin molds.
5. Place molds on a wire rack and bake at 325 F for 20 minutes.
6. Serve and enjoy.

Nutritional Value (Amount per Serving):

- Calories 215
- Fat 19 g
- Carbohydrates 5 g
- Sugar 2 g
- Protein 7 g
- Cholesterol 45 mg

Moist Peanut Butter Muffins

Preparation Time: 10 minutes
Cooking Time: 20 minutes
Serve: 12

Ingredients:

- 1 cup peanut butter
- 1/2 cup maple syrup
- 1 tsp baking soda
- 1 tsp vanilla
- 1/2 cup of cocoa powder
- 1 cup applesauce

Directions:

1. Line 12-cups muffin tin with cupcake liners and set aside.
2. Add all ingredients into the blender and blend until smooth.
3. Pour blended mixture into the prepared muffin tin.
4. Place muffin tin on a wire rack and bake at 350 F for 20 minutes.
5. Serve and enjoy.

Nutritional Value (Amount per Serving):

- Calories 178
- Fat 11.3 g
- Carbohydrates 17.3 g
- Sugar 12 g
- Protein 6.1 g
- Cholesterol 0 mg

Coconut Pie

Preparation Time: 10 minutes
Cooking Time: 12 minutes
Serve: 6

Ingredients:

- 2 eggs
- 1 1/2 tsp vanilla
- 1/2 cup coconut flour
- 1/2 cup Swerve
- 1 cup shredded coconut
- 1/4 cup butter
- 1 1/2 cups coconut milk

Directions:

1. Spray a 6-inch baking dish with cooking spray and set aside.
2. Add all ingredients into the large bowl and mix until well combined.
3. Pour batter into the prepared dish.
4. Place baking dish on a wire rack and bake at 350 F for 12 minutes.
5. Slice and serve.

Nutritional Value (Amount per Serving):

- Calories 317
- Fat 28.9 g
- Carbohydrates 32.3 g
- Sugar 23.1 g
- Protein 5.1 g
- Cholesterol 75 mg

Delicious Cream Cheese Muffins

Preparation Time: 10 minutes
Cooking Time: 16 minutes
Serve: 10

Ingredients:

- 2 eggs
- 1 tsp ground cinnamon
- 1/2 tsp vanilla
- 1/2 cup erythritol
- 8 oz cream cheese

Directions:

1. Insert wire rack in rack position 6. Select bake, set temperature 325 F, timer for 16 minutes. Press start to preheat the oven.
2. In a bowl, mix together cream cheese, vanilla, erythritol, and eggs until soft.
3. Pour batter into the silicone muffin molds and sprinkle cinnamon on top.
4. Cook for 16 minutes.
5. Serve and enjoy.

Nutritional Value (Amount per Serving):

- Calories 90
- Fat 8.8 g
- Carbohydrates 13 g
- Sugar 12.2 g
- Protein 2.8 g
- Cholesterol 58 mg

Pumpkin Cookies

Preparation Time: 10 minutes
Cooking Time: 25 minutes
Serve: 25

Ingredients:

- 1 egg
- 1 tsp vanilla
- 1/2 cup butter
- 1/2 cup pumpkin puree
- 2 cups almond flour
- 1 tsp liquid stevia
- 1/2 tsp pumpkin pie spice
- 1/2 tsp baking powder

Directions:

1. In a large bowl, add all ingredients and mix until well combined.
2. Make 25 cookies from the mixture and place them onto a mesh tray and bake at 320 F for 25 minutes.
3. Serve and enjoy.

Nutritional Value (Amount per Serving):

- Calories 46
- Fat 4.6 g
- Carbohydrates 0.9 g
- Sugar 0.3 g
- Protein 0.7 g
- Cholesterol 15 mg

Chocolate Brownies

Preparation Time: 10 minutes
Cooking Time: 35 minutes
Serve: 9

Ingredients:

- 2 eggs
- 2/3 cup unsweetened cocoa powder
- 2 avocados, mashed
- 2 tbsp swerve
- 1 tsp baking powder
- 4 tbsp coconut oil, melted
- 1/3 cup chocolate chips, melted

Directions:

1. In a mixing bowl, mix together all dry ingredients.
2. In a medium bowl, mix together avocado and eggs until well combined.
3. Add dry mixture to the wet along with melted chocolate and oil. Mix well.
4. Pour batter into a baking dish.
5. Place baking dish on a wire rack and bake at 325 F for 35 minutes.
6. Slice and serve.

Nutritional Value (Amount per Serving):

- Calories 207
- Fat 18 g
- Carbohydrates 11 g
- Sugar 3.6 g
- Protein 3.8 g
- Cholesterol 38 mg

Cream Cheese Muffins

Preparation Time: 10 minutes
Cooking Time: 16 minutes
Serve: 10

Ingredients:

- 2 eggs
- 1 tsp ground cinnamon
- 1/2 tsp vanilla
- 1/2 cup erythritol
- 8 oz cream cheese

Directions:

1. In a bowl, mix together cream cheese, vanilla, erythritol, and eggs until soft.
2. Pour batter into the silicone muffin molds and sprinkle cinnamon on top.
3. Place muffin molds on a wire rack and bake at 325 F for 16 minutes.
4. Serve and enjoy.

Nutritional Value (Amount per Serving):

- Calories 90
- Fat 8.8 g
- Carbohydrates 13 g
- Sugar 12.2 g
- Protein 2.8 g
- Cholesterol 58 mg

Baked Spiced Apples

Preparation Time: 10 minutes
Cooking Time: 10 minutes
Serve: 6

Ingredients:

- 4 apples, sliced
- 1/2 cup erythritol
- 2 tbsp butter, melted
- 1 tsp apple pie spice

Directions:

1. Insert wire rack in rack position 6. Select bake, set temperature 350 F, timer for 10 minutes. Press start to preheat the oven.
2. Add apple slices in a large bowl and sprinkle with sweetener and apple pie spice. Add melted butter and toss to coat.
3. Transfer apple slices in a baking dish and air fry for 10 minutes.
4. Serve and enjoy.

Nutritional Value (Amount per Serving):

- Calories 73
- Fat 4.6 g
- Carbohydrates 8.2 g
- Sugar 5.4 g
- Protein 0 g
- Cholesterol 0 mg

Almond Cinnamon Muffins

Preparation Time: 10 minutes
Cooking Time: 12 minutes
Serve: 20

Ingredients:

- 1/2 cup almond flour
- 1/2 cup coconut oil
- 1/2 cup pumpkin puree
- 1 tbsp cinnamon
- 1 tsp baking powder
- 2 scoops vanilla protein powder
- 1/2 cup almond butter

Directions:

1. Insert wire rack in rack position 6. Select air fry, set temperature 325 F, timer for 12 minutes. Press start to preheat the oven.
2. In a large bowl, mix together all dry ingredients.
3. Add wet ingredients into the dry ingredients and mix until well combined.
4. Pour batter into the silicone muffin molds and cook for 12 minutes.
5. Serve and enjoy.

Nutritional Value (Amount per Serving):

- Calories 80
- Fat 7.1 g
- Carbohydrates 1 g
- Sugar 0.4 g
- Protein 3 g
- Cholesterol 0 mg

Healthy Blueberry Muffins

Preparation Time: 10 minutes
Cooking Time: 20 minutes
Serve: 12

Ingredients:

- 3 large eggs
- 2 1/2 cups almond flour
- 3/4 cup blueberries
- 1/2 tsp vanilla
- 1/3 cup almond milk
- 1/3 cup coconut oil, melted
- 1 1/2 tsp gluten-free baking powder
- 1/2 cup erythritol

Directions:

1. Insert wire rack in rack position 6. Select air fry, set temperature 325 F, timer for 20 minutes. Press start to preheat the oven.
2. In a large bowl, mix together almond flour, baking powder, erythritol.
3. Stir in the coconut oil, vanilla, eggs, and almond milk.
4. Add blueberries and fold well.
5. Pour batter into the silicone muffin molds and cook muffins for 20 minutes.
6. Serve and enjoy.

Nutritional Value (Amount per Serving):

- Calories 215
- Fat 19 g
- Carbohydrates 5 g
- Sugar 2 g
- Protein 7 g
- Cholesterol 45 mg

Baked Apples

Preparation Time: 10 minutes
Cooking Time: 10 minutes
Serve: 6

Ingredients:

- 4 apples, sliced
- 2 tbsp butter, melted
- 1 tsp apple pie spice
- 1/2 cup erythritol

Directions:

1. Add apple slices in a large bowl and sprinkle with sweetener and apple pie spice.
2. Add melted butter and toss to coat.
3. Transfer apple slices in a baking dish.
4. Place baking dish on a wire rack and bake at 350 F for 10 minutes.
5. Serve and enjoy.

Nutritional Value (Amount per Serving):

- Calories 73
- Fat 4.6 g
- Carbohydrates 8.2 g
- Sugar 5.4 g
- Protein 0 g
- Cholesterol 0 mg

Raspberry Cobbler

Preparation Time: 10 minutes
Cooking Time: 10 minutes
Serve: 6

Ingredients:

- 1 egg, lightly beaten
- 1 cup raspberries, sliced
- 2 tsp swerve
- 1/2 tsp vanilla
- 1 tbsp butter, melted
- 1 cup almond flour

Directions:

1. Add raspberries to the baking dish.
2. Sprinkle sweetener over raspberries.
3. Mix together almond flour, vanilla, and butter in the bowl.
4. Add egg in almond flour mixture and stir well to combine.
5. Spread almond flour mixture over sliced raspberries.
6. Place baking dish on a wire rack and bake at 350 F for 10 minutes.
7. Serve and enjoy.

Nutritional Value (Amount per Serving):

- Calories 66
- Fat 5 g
- Carbohydrates 3 g
- Sugar 1 g
- Protein 2 g
- Cholesterol 32 mg

Cheesecake

Preparation Time: 10minutes
Cooking Time: 10 minutes
Serve: 2

Ingredients:

- 2 eggs
- 16 oz cream cheese, softened
- 2 tbsp sour cream
- 1/2 tsp fresh lemon juice
- 1 tsp vanilla
- 3/4 cup Swerve

Directions:

1. Insert wire rack in rack position 6. Select air fry, set temperature 350 F, timer for 10 minutes. Press start to preheat the oven.
2. Add eggs, lemon juice, vanilla, and sweetener in a large bowl and beat until smooth.
3. Add cream cheese and sour cream and beat until fluffy.
4. Pour batter into the 2 4-inch springform pan and cook for 10 minutes.
5. Place in refrigerator overnight.
6. Serve and enjoy.

Nutritional Value (Amount per Serving):

- Calories 886
- Fat 86 g
- Carbohydrates 97.2 g
- Sugar 91.1 g
- Protein 23.1 g
- Cholesterol 418 mg

Moist Chocolate Brownies

Preparation Time: 10 minutes
Cooking Time: 35 minutes
Serve: 9

Ingredients:

- 2 eggs
- 1 tsp baking powder
- 4 tbsp coconut oil, melted
- 2/3 cup unsweetened cocoa powder
- 2 avocados, mashed
- 2 tbsp swerve
- 1/3 cup chocolate chips, melted

Directions:

1. Insert wire rack in rack position 6. Select bake, set temperature 325 F, timer for 35 minutes. Press start to preheat the oven.
2. In a mixing bowl, mix together all dry ingredients.
3. In another bowl, mix together avocado and eggs until well combined.
4. Add dry mixture to the wet along with melted chocolate and oil. Mix well.
5. Pour batter in a baking dish and bake for 35 minutes.
6. Slice and serve.

Nutritional Value (Amount per Serving):

- Calories 207
- Fat 18 g
- Carbohydrates 11 g
- Sugar 3.6 g
- Protein 3.8 g
- Cholesterol 38 mg

Vanilla Coconut Pie

Preparation Time: 10 minutes
Cooking Time: 12 minutes
Serve: 6

Ingredients:

- 2 eggs
- 1 1/2 tsp vanilla
- 1/4 cup butter
- 1 1/2 cups coconut milk
- 1/2 cup coconut flour
- 1/2 cup Swerve
- 1 cup shredded coconut

Directions:

1. Spray a 6-inch baking dish with cooking spray and set aside.
2. Insert wire rack in rack position 6. Select bake, set temperature 350 F, timer for 12 minutes. Press start to preheat the oven.
3. Add all ingredients into the large bowl and mix until well combined.
4. Pour batter into the prepared dish and cook for 10-12 minutes.
5. Slice and serve.

Nutritional Value (Amount per Serving):

- Calories 317
- Fat 28.9 g
- Carbohydrates 32.3 g
- Sugar 23.1 g
- Protein 5.1 g
- Cholesterol 75 mg

Almond Muffins

Preparation Time: 10 minutes
Cooking Time: 20 minutes
Serve: 12

Ingredients:

- 4 eggs
- 1 tsp baking soda
- 1 orange zest
- 1 orange juice
- 1/2 cup butter, melted
- 3 cups almond flour

Directions:

1. Line 12-cups muffin tin with cupcake liners and set aside.
2. Add all ingredients into the large bowl and mix until well combined.
3. Pour mixture into the prepared muffin tin.
4. Place muffin tin on a wire rack and bake at 350 F for 20 minutes.
5. Serve and enjoy.

Nutritional Value (Amount per Serving):

- Calories 273
- Fat 24 g
- Carbohydrates 6 g
- Sugar 1 g
- Protein 2 g
- Cholesterol 75 mg

Choco Lava Cake

Preparation Time: 10 minutes
Cooking Time: 9 minutes
Serve: 2

Ingredients:

- 1 egg
- 1/2 tsp baking powder
- 2 tbsp water
- 2 tbsp cocoa powder
- 1 tbsp butter, melted
- 1 tbsp flax meal
- 2 tbsp Swerve
- Pinch of salt

Directions:

1. Spray 2 ramekins with cooking spray and set aside.
2. Insert wire rack in rack position 6. Select air fry, set temperature 350 F, timer for 9 minutes. Press start to preheat the oven.
3. In a bowl, whisk together all ingredients until well combined.
4. Pour batter into the prepared ramekins and bake for 9 minutes.
5. Serve and enjoy.

Nutritional Value (Amount per Serving):

- Calories 121
- Fat 11 g
- Carbohydrates 19.9 g
- Sugar 15.3 g
- Protein 4.6 g
- Cholesterol 82 mg

Almond Pumpkin Muffins

Preparation Time: 10 minutes
Cooking Time: 20 minutes
Serve: 10

Ingredients:

- 4 large eggs
- 2/3 cup erythritol
- 1 tsp vanilla
- 1/3 cup coconut oil, melted
- 1/2 cup almond flour
- 1/2 cup pumpkin puree
- 1 tbsp pumpkin pie spice
- 1 tbsp baking powder
- 1/2 cup coconut flour
- 1/2 tsp sea salt

Directions:

1. Insert wire rack in rack position 6. Select air fry, set temperature 325 F, timer for 20 minutes. Press start to preheat the oven.
2. In a large bowl, mix together coconut flour, pumpkin pie spice, baking powder, erythritol, almond flour, and sea salt.
3. Stir in eggs, vanilla, coconut oil, and pumpkin puree until well combined.
4. Pour batter into the silicone muffin molds and cook muffins for 20 minutes.
5. Serve and enjoy.

Nutritional Value (Amount per Serving):

- Calories 150
- Fat 13 g
- Carbohydrates 7 g
- Sugar 2 g
- Protein 5 g

- Cholesterol 75 mg

Choco Almond Butter Brownie

Preparation Time: 10 minutes
Cooking Time: 16 minutes
Serve: 4

Ingredients:

- 1 cup bananas, overripe
- 1/2 cup almond butter, melted
- 1 scoop protein powder
- 2 tbsp cocoa powder

Directions:

1. Insert wire rack in rack position 6. Select air fry, set temperature 350 F, timer for 16 minutes. Press start to preheat the oven.
2. Spray baking dish with cooking spray.
3. Add all ingredients into the blender and blend until smooth.
4. Pour batter into the prepared baking dish and cook brownie for 16 minutes.
5. Serve and enjoy.

Nutritional Value (Amount per Serving):

- Calories 80
- Fat 2.1 g
- Carbohydrates 11.4 g
- Protein 7 g
- Sugars 5 g
- Cholesterol 15 mg

Peanut Butter Cake

Preparation Time: 10 minutes
Cooking Time: 30 minutes
Serve: 8

Ingredients:

- 1 1/2 cups all-purpose flour
- 1/2 cup peanut butter powder
- 1 tsp vanilla
- 1 tbsp apple cider vinegar
- 1/3 cup vegetable oil
- 1 tsp baking soda
- 1 cup of water
- 1 cup of sugar
- 1/2 tsp salt

Directions:

1. In a large mixing bowl, mix together flour, baking soda, peanut butter powder, sugar, and salt.
2. In a small bowl, whisk together oil, vanilla, vinegar, and water.
3. Pour oil mixture into the flour mixture and stir until well combined.
4. Pour batter into the greased cake pan.
5. Place cake pan on a wire rack and bake at 350 F for 30 minutes.
6. Slice and serve.

Nutritional Value (Amount per Serving):

- Calories 264
- Fat 1.8 g
- Carbohydrates 43.2 g
- Sugar 25.3 g
- Protein 2.6 g
- Cholesterol 0 mg

Chapter 9: 30-Day Meal Plan

Day 1

Breakfast- Italian Frittata

Lunch- Tasty Cajun Shrimp

Dinner- Chili Garlic Chicken Wings

Day 2

Breakfast- Broccoli Quiche

Lunch- Shrimp Casserole

Dinner- Chicken Casserole

Day 3

Breakfast- Italian Frittata

Lunch- Garlic Tomato Shrimp

Dinner- Tarragon Chicken

Day 4

Breakfast- Broccoli Quiche

Lunch- Rosemary Shrimp

Dinner- Ranch Pork Chops

Day 5

Breakfast- Tasty Baked Eggs

Lunch- Spicy Shrimp

Dinner- Lamb Patties

Day 6

Breakfast- Egg Cheese Casserole

Lunch- Greek Scallops

Dinner- Rosemary Pork Chops

Day 7

Breakfast- Baked Egg Muffins

Lunch- Spicy Salmon

Dinner- Pork Tenderloin

Day 8

Breakfast- Pumpkin Bread

Lunch- Dijon Salmon

Dinner- Rosemary Pork Chops

Day 9

Breakfast- Blueberry Oatmeal

Lunch- Baked Lemon Butter Cod

Dinner- Tasty Parmesan Pork Chops

Day 10

Breakfast- Ham Egg Casserole

Lunch- Scallop Gratin

Dinner- Pork Tenderloin

Day 11

Breakfast- Banana Bread

Lunch- Baked Chicken Breasts

Dinner- Tasty Parmesan Pork Chops

Day 12

Breakfast- Oat Squash Muffins

Lunch- Chicken Patties

Dinner- Garlic Butter Pork Chops

Day 13

Breakfast- Ham Egg Casserole

Lunch- Lemon Pepper Chicken

Dinner- Juicy Pork Chops

Day 14

Breakfast- Italian Frittata

Lunch- Baked Turkey Breast

Dinner- Tasty Parmesan Pork Chops

Day 15

Breakfast- Oat Squash Muffins

Lunch- Dijon Chicken Thighs

Dinner- Creamy Pork Chops

Day 16

Breakfast- Italian Frittata

Lunch- Tasty Cajun Shrimp

Dinner- Chili Garlic Chicken Wings

Day 17

Breakfast- Broccoli Quiche

Lunch- Shrimp Casserole

Dinner- Chicken Casserole

Day 18

Breakfast- Italian Frittata

Lunch- Garlic Tomato Shrimp

Dinner- Tarragon Chicken

Day 19

Breakfast- Broccoli Quiche

Lunch- Rosemary Shrimp

Dinner- Ranch Pork Chops

Day 20

Breakfast- Tasty Baked Eggs

Lunch- Spicy Shrimp

Dinner- Lamb Patties

Day 21

Breakfast- Egg Cheese Casserole

Lunch- Greek Scallops

Dinner- Rosemary Pork Chops

Day 22

Breakfast- Baked Egg Muffins

Lunch- Spicy Salmon

Dinner- Pork Tenderloin

Day 23

Breakfast- Pumpkin Bread

Lunch- Dijon Salmon

Dinner- Rosemary Pork Chops

Day 24

Breakfast- Blueberry Oatmeal

Lunch- Baked Lemon Butter Cod

Dinner- Tasty Parmesan Pork Chops

Day 25

Breakfast- Ham Egg Casserole

Lunch- Scallop Gratin

Dinner- Pork Tenderloin

Day 26

Breakfast- Banana Bread

Lunch- Baked Chicken Breasts

Dinner- Tasty Parmesan Pork Chops

Day 27

Breakfast- Oat Squash Muffins

Lunch- Chicken Patties

Dinner- Garlic Butter Pork Chops

Day 28

Breakfast- Ham Egg Casserole

Lunch- Lemon Pepper Chicken

Dinner- Juicy Pork Chops

Day 29

Breakfast- Italian Frittata

Lunch- Baked Turkey Breast

Dinner- Tasty Parmesan Pork Chops

Day 30

Breakfast- Oat Squash Muffins

Lunch- Dijon Chicken Thighs

Dinner- Creamy Pork Chops

Conclusion

If you are still worrying about what to eat every day, you should first buy the most suitable oven on the market. You need to know how they make delicious food and how they work. Calphalon performance air fry convection oven are cleaner and more hygienic than those on the market. If you buy it, you will experience the feeling of being a chef and get a sense of happiness, and have a healthier, delicious and convenient diet.

Calphalon performance air fry convection oven that combines the advantages of air frying pan and oven provides a great cooking experience with everyone, making food taste better and cooking easier.

www.ingramcontent.com/pod-product-compliance
Lightning Source LLC
LaVergne TN
LVHW081822270125
802311LV00008B/211
* 9 7 8 1 9 5 4 7 0 3 5 3 7 *